KIDS AND ALCOHOL

Facts and Ideas about
DRINKING AND NOT DRINKING

Written by:
Jamie Rattray,
Bill Howells and Irv Siegler
Illustrated by:
Fritz Wasser

September 1982 — Revised 1984
Health Communications, Inc.
2119-A Hollywood Boulevard
Hollywood, Florida 33020

ISBN 0-932194-13-3

Published by Health Communications, Inc.
2119-A Hollywood Blvd., Hollywood, FLorida 33020

TABLE OF CONTENTS

Acknowledgments

The authors would like to thank our employer, the Corning-Painted Post Area School District, and the Corning Area Council on Alcoholism (Corning, New York), for having the foresight and courage to allow us to develop the **KIDS AND ALCOHOL** portion of the **"Get High on Life"** series. We would also like to show our appreciation to our many colleagues for their time and energy spent in piloting, implementing and evaluating this book. Special recognition is given to Anthony J. DiBenedetto, Bureau Chief of Drug Education (New York State Education Department) and to Chuck Nelson, Health Risk Reduction Program director (New York State Health Department) for their constant support and encouragement.

Acknowledgment is paid to Abt Associates, Inc., Cambridge, Mass., for permission to rewrite portions of **KIDS AND ALCOHOL** (1976). It was this original text which was written by Peter Finn and Jane Lawson with graphics by Linda W. Clement that inspired us to develop the **"Get High on Life"** series.

Acknowledgment is paid to University Associates of San Diego, Calif., for permission to incorporate the "valuing process" originally published in **Advanced Value Clarification** written by Howard Kirschenbaum, Ed.D. (1977), and to the Addiction Research Foundation, Toronto, Ontario, Canada, for permission to reprint "This Book Belongs to ... " from **It's My Life** (1976).

CHAPTER 0

A WORD FROM THE GURU

There are two kinds of people in this world: **victims and choosers.** Victims are controlled by what other people may say and do. Choosers make decisions for themselves. They set goals and try to reach those goals. They are problem-solvers, and they **take pride in themselves.**

You know . . .

Life is full of problems and anxieties, and being human means experiencing good times and bad. We all need to learn how to face problems because sometimes things do not turn out the way we expect or hope them to—or want them to. But, we don't have to accept everything that happens to us. There are even certain **problems which you can prevent** from ever happening by simply avoiding certain situations. **You can choose to think for yourself.** No one can make you do anything!

You will not always be able to foresee the consequences of your behavior, and there will be times when you will not be in complete control of certain situations. This is particularly true while you are young and dependent on others. As you grow older, you will be held **responsible for your own behavior**, and for this reason it is paramount that you understand the mechanics of decision-making.

The theme of **KIDS AND ALCOHOL** is **Get High on Life.** I hope that reading this book will help you make some of the important decisions in your life—help you learn to feel good about yourself; who you are and what you do.

Just remember, living life to its fullest means taking risks, but you don't "only go 'round once in life ..." You go 'round every day. Enjoy your life! Work and play hard! **Become a chooser—not a victim.**

As you read and work through **KIDS AND ALCOHOL**, you will run across places where there are questions. As you come to these, there will be spaces provided for you to write your answers—how you feel, what you believe to be true, and so on. (You can even check your answers on the pages following the questions.)

At times in this book you will come upon **questions** to which there are **no right or wrong answers**. You will probably want to discuss some of the questions in class or with an adult at home.

Many activities are provided throughout this book. These are meant to challenge you with additional opportunities to get involved in other enjoyable aspects of learning. I hope you find **KIDS AND ALCOHOL** to be informative, thought-provoking, and enjoyable (maybe even funny at times).

Sincerely,

bumper

CHAPTER 1

VALUES, DECISIONS AND YOU!

Decide For Yourself!

This little book has two purposes—first, to help you **learn about alcohol**, and second, to help you **learn how to attain control of your own life.**

In this portion of our book we will be looking at how you can develop skills which will help you make responsible decisions and feel good about them. Pay attention! (Or else we'll tell all your friends that you sleep with a frog under your pillow.)

Hopefully, we will also help you decide **how alcohol fits into your life**—a decision which is up to you. (Maybe you can discuss some of these ideas at home . . .)

Taking Control!

As people grow, they are able to increase the amount of control they have over their lives, and to increase their ability to make decisions according to:

- What they want ...
- What they feel is important ...
- What they value ...
- What they expect will happen in their lives ...

People who expect something positive in their lives take control of their lives. They set goals, and they try to obtain those goals. We call this positive self-expectation, and this is very important in decision-making.

A baby can't make many decisions, except for simple reactions (like spitting out spinach). This is because of a lack of knowledge, experience, and poor communication skills. But . . .

You Can!

Kids your age can make more decisions, or at least try to, because you have more knowledge, experience, and can **communicate your ideas** and desires better. You can choose your food, clothing, friends ... and **make other decisions based on your choices** (what you *want*).

Of course, many of your choices are limited by other people in your life (like your parents, teachers, and goldfish).

As You Get Older . . .

You will be making many more decisions in all areas. The number of social choices for you to make will be especially large—who your friends are, what you do for entertainment, what school subjects you will take, how much education you want or need, and other stuff like that.

Growing Up!

As you finish school (and/or grow up), you will have the largest number of choices—and some of your decisions will have much more **serious consequences.** (Look up "consequences" in your handy, dandy pocket dictionary, if you don't know what that means.)

You'll be making decisions that affect your life, career, marriage, etc.—and these decisions will be harder to make . . .

Sooo . . .

You can see that making decisions is something that must be learned and practiced. As you grow older, you become more and more responsible for **making decisions** and for accepting the **consequences** (see—we told you to look it up).

In this book we want to help you **develop a process** that you can use to make the best possible decisions, to realize **why** you do what you do, and to make sure that you are giving yourself the best shot at doing what **you want to do.**

PS-E!

The above initials stand for **positive self-expectation**—something we hope you will learn to develop. Since we want you to begin to expect something positive will result from reading this book, we suggest that you peek ahead to page 187 (Activity No. 73). It's okay. Go ahead and peek.

Making Decisions

There are many ways that people make decisions.

- Some people **choose to allow other people to decide for them.**
- Some people **choose to allow fate, luck, etc. to decide for them.**
- Some people **choose not to make a decision.**

We hope that you will choose to make decisions (especially important ones), based on a well-thought-out-method. Here's how ...

Developing Values

When you have **a strong feeling that something is important, it is called a value**. Values are personal, and they depend on your individual beliefs. A few examples of values for people might include ...

- Taking pride in your appearance
- Trying to do the best you can (on a project—a job—in school, sports, etc.)
- Being fair and honest
- Developing positive self-expectation

Hopefully, your values are those things which make you feel good about yourself. **Developing values** is one of the main ideas throughout this book.

Controlling Your Life

There is something called **the valuing process** which we will use to help you decide how you feel about some things. However, there will be no attempt to force you to believe something—this decision is the one you will have to make for yourself. For example, **we won't tell you whether you should or shouldn't drink alcohol**. What we *will* do is to provide you with some guidelines that could help you **make that decision for yourself** (help you control your own life).

The valuing process has five steps which answer these questions:

(1) THINKING	What's happening?
(2) FEELING	How do I feel about what's happening?
(3) CHOOSING	What choices do I have? What are the consequences of each choice?
(4) COMMUNICATING ...	Does what I *mean* come through in what I say and do? Am I really listening to others?
(5) ACTING	Do my actions come as a result of my thoughts, feelings, and choices?

Study these five steps and try to learn them. If you don't, your belly-button will fall out!

The basic idea behind the valuing process is to enable you to examine at least **three alternatives** to any problem situation before you make a decision.

This symbol will be used throughout this book. Whenever you see it, you will know that the **valuing process discussion rules** are in effect.

VALUING PROCESS DISCUSSION RULES

1. Nobody puts down anybody else for what they say. No judgments.
2. There aren't any right or wrong answers or attitudes.
3. Just one person can speak at a time. No one can interrupt.
4. If you choose not to answer, simply say, "I pass."
5. You may change your mind at any time.

Congratulations!!

You've made it through the reading part of this chapter! Now let's put what you read to work. Let's see if you can try to use the valuing process in the following made-up situation.

Pretend that you've just received a letter from a friend about a problem that she has. Let's try to work through the steps of the valuing process together before you help your friend with her problem.

The Problem . . .

This is the part of the letter you received which explains the problem:

> Sometimes when I get together with my three friends, one of them gets his older brother to get beer for us. Since one of us usually has nobody home on any night, we go over to that house to drink. Sometimes my friends drink a lot and get drunk. Since I don't like to drink, I try to drink very little—but they keep pushing me to drink more. I know that if I get caught I'll be grounded for months; and I really don't like to drink. BUT these are my best friends. What should I do?

This is a tough one! Let's see if we can work on it using the steps from **page 17**. Turn to the next page and we'll get you started.

How To ...

There are several methods of using the valuing process. We'll show you two ways (you're a smart kid who can think up more ways if you want to).

One way is to list all the known facts which should be considered before making a decision.

A second way is to list questions about the problem situation and try to answer them.

On the next two pages, we've given examples of these lists for steps 1 and 2, THINKING and FEELING.

Look back to **page 21** if you've forgotten the problem.

STEP 1: **THINKING** (What's Happening?)

Facts (Method 1)

- My friends like to get drunk.
- I'm under a lot of pressure from my friends to drink more.
- I'll have a problem at home if my parents find out.
- I don't know if my friends will want me around if I don't drink.

Questions (Method 2)

- Why do my friends want to get drunk?
- Can (should) I resist my friends' pressure?
- What will happen if my parents find out?
- How will my friends act toward me if I don't drink?

STEP 2: **FEELING** (How Do You Feel About What's Happening?)

Facts

- I don't feel comfortable drinking in one of our houses when nobody else is there.
- It bothers me that my friends try to get me to do things I don't like.
- It would disappoint my parents and probably make them very angry if they found out.
- My friends are important to me and I dont' want to lose them.

Questions

- How do I feel about not having permission to drink and being trusted — and drinking anyway?
- How do I feel when my friends pressure me to do things I don't like?
- How would my parents feel if they found out?
- Will I lose my friends if I don't go along with them?

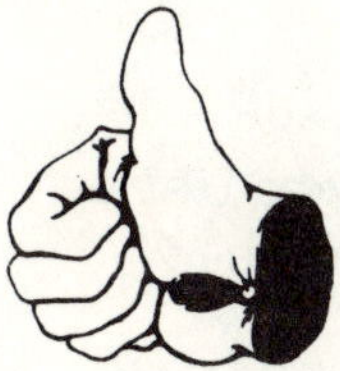

Activity No. 23, Brainstorm Some Ideas ...

See if you can add to these lists for **steps 1 and 2** by yourself, or in small groups.

Remember to follow **the valuing process discussion rules** while you work with others. **See page 19.**

Also remember, we're not making a choice yet; what we're doing is trying to understand the problem.

STEP 3: **CHOOSING** (What Choices Do I Have? What Are The Consequences of Each?)

Remember our problem (**page 21**). Now, by yourself, try to list as many choices as you can. Try for at least three more. What would happen as a result of each choice?

Choices	Results
1. I could tell my friends I'm not going to drink any more.	**1.** They might drop me.
2.	**2.**
3.	**3.**
4.	**4.**

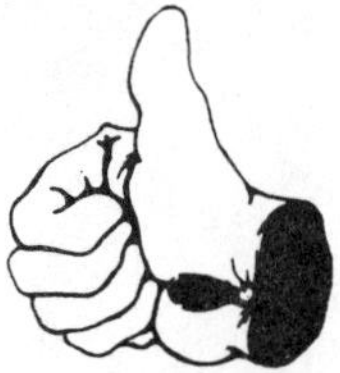

STEP 4: COMMUNICATING (Does My Meaning Come Through? Am I Listening?)

Discuss the choices you just listed in **step 3** with a small group of your classmates. Remember, the **valuing process discussion rules** are in effect.

Thought Question

What would you do if you had a problem like this?

"I think . . . ____

____

____."

STEP 5: ACTING (Is This What I Really Should Do?)

Write below the solution you would suggest to your friend to solve her problem. Notice that now **you have made a decision.**

____

____

____

____

____

____

We hope . . .

If you had a friend with a big problem like that, we hope you would help him/her go through the decision process and help solve the problem.

Remember earlier we talked about positive self-expectation (page 13)? How do you think **PS-E** fits into your friend's problem?

"I think . . . ____

____

____."

Heads or Tails?

Some decisions need to be really thought-out (like our make-believe problem). Other decisions are much easier to make. When people don't take time to think about the consequences of their decisions before acting, then they may feel sorry later for what they did or said.

Did you ever think "I wish I hadn't done that," or "Why did I say that?" **Following our decision process can help avoid this problem** (and it looks classier than just flipping a coin).

Thinking and Deciding!

Throughout this book—and your life—we hope that the valuing process you've just gone through will help you in making decisions. Remember—**many decisions that you do make are not simply "yes" or "no" situations**. Some decisions you will have to make will require a great deal of thought. You will find that even after thinking and using the step-by-step process, it is still difficult to make the right decision.

You may wish to spend some time discussing how you know if a decision is the right one. Maybe you could talk to your parents about this, and ask them how they make certain decisions. How do they know if they have made the right decision?

Here Are Some More Amazing Thoughts That You Should Be Aware Of About Decisions

1. **When you make a decision, you are responsible for the decision.** If you change your mind, that new decision is also your responsibility. Remember, sometimes you can't change your mind (like after you're in too deep to get out).

2. The older you get the more decisions you'll have to make ... Sorry, that's part of growing up. As you grow older, these decisions will probably involve additional risks.

Taking risks is one thing that makes life interesting and helps you to grow. If you never took any risks, life would be pretty empty and boring and safe. But we all take risks — that's one way we learn. Sometimes we make mistakes when we reach for a goal which is attractive, but we decide to accept the risks involved.

Taking risks from time to time can help you have a full and rewarding life, especially if they are carefully considered risks.

Some people take foolish and unnecessary risks. They take chances and make decisions which put their health and lives in danger. This is not highly recommended.

3. Sometimes people make a decision based on having fun or feeling good right now without thinking of future results. You may not be able to foresee **all the consequences,** but if you follow our process and ...

- Look at each decision
- Think about at least **three** choices and what results they might have
- Be clear about what you mean
- Then act accordingly ...

You have a better chance of not making a choice that could have disasterous effects on your life.

Also . . .

4. When you do nothing about a problem, then you really have done something. **You have decided to allow fate or other people to control your life.** Even if you decide to let others make your decisions for you, **you** still have to take the responsibility for those decisions.

5. One final word about making decisions. You have a great deal of **freedom** in making decisions. **When you make a personal decision you choose from a number of possible actions** — and the more possible choices you give yourself, the freer your choice really is. So it is very important for you to examine as many choices as you can, and to make a decision based on your own goals and predictions.

When you make good decisions people will trust you more — and when that happens you will be given even more control over your own life and more choices to make.

> Remember — if you can carefully examine your values and choices relating to a problem situation before making your decision, you will probably feel confident about the action you decide to take, and **that's what life's all about — feeling good about yourself!**

CHAPTER 2

ALCOHOL: FACTS AND FALSEHOODS!

We've dedicated this chapter to the idea that: **What we know, or think we know ...**

. . . can really hurt us!

This portion of the book will help you to explore many of the **fictions, falsehoods, fables, fibs, fantasies** and **frauds**, which surround alcohol and drinking. Why do we care to write a chapter about stuff that's not true? Easy . . .because we don't know the truth — Ha ha.

Seriously Folks ...

The **false ideas** that many people have about drinking have **hurt** all of **us.** You know, there are over nine million alcoholics in this country. Many people who drink have the wrong idea about what they're drinking and why.

Sooo . . . the more we know about alcohol and drinking the better we'll be able to make **responsible decisions about drinking**. And that's what this book is all about.

Pay Attention to This Stuff!

Or else you have to go back to first grade, and you won't get to take the final exam.

We hope that the following few pages will help straighten out some common misunderstandings about drinking. It will be a real eye-opener for you to discuss some of these false ideas with others — especially an adult at home.

Where does alcohol fit in your life???

True or False?

It doesn't matter how much you drink, as long as you stick to beer?

True or False? ____________________

FALSE (Of Course!)

One can of beer has about the same amount of alcohol as a glass of wine or a shot of hard liquor. It might take a longer time, but you'll get just as drunk on beer as you will on wine or hard liquor.

"I better drive home — I'm too drunk to walk!" (**WRONG!!!**)

Mid-Chapter Low Intelligence Achievement Test

How many ounces of beer are in your basic beer can? (Circle One)

A. 12
B. 6 = 6
C. None, because it's empty.
D. Some of the above.

ANSWER — E.

TRUE OR FALSE?

It is a sign of being grown-up to be able to drink a great amount.

True or False? ____________________

FALSE AGAIN!

There is nothing grown-up about drinking a lot, or in out-drinking your friends. It is as foolish to over-drink as it is to over-eat . . . and it is just as unhealthy.

TRUE OR FALSE?

Alcohol is most commonly used by older people. Today's kids use other drugs instead of alcohol.

True or False? ____________________

FALSE (What Else?)

The widely talked-about generation gap doesn't extend to alcohol. Kids and adults share a common drug—**alcohol**. And the really bad news—drinking problems are increasing among the young.

TRUE OR FALSE?

Being drunk — and getting drunk is really funny.

True or False? ____________________

FALSE You Say? Right Again!

Unlike what you see in many old movies and cartoons on T.V., there is nothing humorous about drunkenness in real life. It is about as funny as any other serious illness or handicap.

TRUE OR FALSE?

What really gets a person drunk or super sick is switching drinks (like starting with 3-4 beers, then having some wine).

True or False? ____________________

FALSE Again! (Are you getting the picture?)

Switching really doesn't make that much difference. What does make a difference is the amount of alcohol a person drinks!

TRUE OR FALSE?

When people are drunk they are friendlier.

True or False? ___________

Is **FALSE** your answer? (You clever little devil!) Sure, some people may get friendlier when they're drunk. Unfortunately some also get meaner, more dangerous, angrier, or even homicidal or suicidal. In fact, alcohol figures into about 50% of all murders (homicides), and about one third of the cases of suicide — and that's not friendly!

TRUE OR FALSE?

Not too many women become alcoholics.

True or False? ______________

FALSE (You got it!)

Unfortunately, the number of women alcoholics compared to men is increasing. In the 1950's, there were five or six male alcoholics to every female alcoholic. Today it is closer to three men to one woman alcoholic. **You've come a long way baby.** (Most women who have come a long way do not want to be called "baby!")

TRUE OR FALSE?

If a person has parents who don't drink, there is no need to worry; their kids won't drink either.

True or False? ____________________

FALSE (You maybe thought otherwise by now?)

Sometimes that holds true — however, statistics show that the highest rates of alcoholism show up among the children of two types of parents: alcoholics and teetotalers (non-drinkers)!

It is just possible that such extreme attitudes and examples shown by parents play a major role in their children's decisions.

TRUE OR FALSE?

As long as you drink with others, and not alone, you don't have to worry about becoming and alcoholic.

True or False? ____________________

FALSE! (Need we tell you?)

Many people who are just so-called social drinkers have real drinking problems. Just because a person never drinks alone doesn't mean he/she can't have a problem with alcohol.

Activity No. 97 "Can You Sell It?"

Get with two or three other kids. Write and act out a short T.V. or radio commercial trying to get people to buy a make-believe alcohol product such as:

- Red wine-flavored peanut butter
- Cocktails for cats and dogs
- Beer Flakes cereal

Try to sell your product by making it seem . . .

Sexy	In	New
Cool	Good for you	Exciting
Glamorous	Cute	Macho

In other words, use the same tricks and techniques that advertising companies use every day!

TRUE OR FALSE?

You're not an alcoholic unless you drink a lot each day (like a pint every day).

True or False? ____________________

False. The amount of drinking isn't the way to tell an alcoholic. There is no set amount. Experts feel that how much people drink may not be nearly as important as . . .

- What they drink
- How they drink
- Why they drink

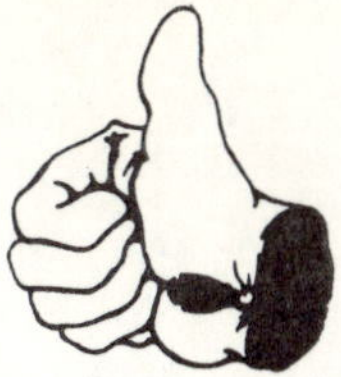

Activity No. 745, Voting on Values

Place a mark in a column to show your feelings about each statement. Discuss in class or at home.

STATEMENT	STRONGLY AGREE	AGREE	DISAGREE	STRONGLY DISAGREE
1. The minimum drinking age should be raised.				
2. The minimum drinking age should be lowered.				
3. I wouldn't want my kids to drink.				
4. I wouldn't ride with a driver who had been drinking.				
5. Alcohol is a drug.				

TRUE OR FALSE?

When you reach the legal drinking age, it is time to start learning about alcohol and its effects.

True or False? ____________

FALSE (Well—you had a 50:50 chance to get it right—don't complain.)
The proper time to **start your education about drinking** is when you start to learn everything else—at birth.
Incidentally, what we see people do (their actions and examples) teaches us a whole lot more than what they tell us. Actions really do speak louder than words!

Facts and Falsehoods Continued ...

You can see by now, that there are a lot of misconceptions that people have about drinking. You have seen that **drinking alcohol affects people in many different ways.** Alcohol may also affect the same person differently, at different times.

How drinking affects you — what it makes you do or feel — depends on things other than just the amount you consume.

Before going on maybe you might want to quiz your parents by asking them some of the questions we just discussed? Don't be surprised if they get some wrong!

How alcohol affects you also depends on . . .

- **Your size** (how heavy you are).
- **Your experience** (how much alcohol you've drunk in the past).
- **Your expectations** (what you think and hope to have alcohol do for you).
- Other things too (these will be discussed in the next chapter).

TRUE OR FALSE?

The way that alcohol affects a person depends largely on these three factors:

1. The person's size
2. The person's experience with alcohol
3. What the person expects alcohol to do for him/her.

True or False? ____________________

TRUE! (You just knew there would be a true one in here someplace!)

If you missed this one, check back on page 66. More about this in the next chapter, too.

FINAL EXAM

Please think carefully—and no peeking. This is your last **TRUE OR FALSE** question in this chapter.

Question: When you know the truth about the possible effects of alcohol, you can make a better decision about how alcohol fits into your life.

True or False? ________________

FINAL EXAM ANSWER

TRUE — and if you missed that one, you should copy this entire chapter in blood (but not your own blood, use blood from an aardvark or somebody from New Jersey).

And Again We Ask . . .
where does alcohol fit into your life? **Only you can decide . . .**

Activity No. 99, Parent Quiz

Take your book home and ask your parents to answer each of the true-false questions in this chapter. Discuss their answers with them.

Perhaps your teacher will give you some sort of extra credit for doing this. Even more important, if you discuss this book and other things like this with your folks, you will get to **know each other** even better than you do now. That beats extra credit any day!

CHAPTER 3

THE EFFECTS OF ALCOHOL!?

How and Why . . .

This portion of your book will explain **how alcohol passes through your body** and **how it affects the drinker** and why.

Study this material carefully (or else we'll put peanut butter in your socks!).

What Happens to Alcohol in Your Body?

Look at the following chart (pages 76-77). If you can follow the dotted lines, you can trace the path alcohol takes in your body. Next to each number you can find a lot of information. You'll see where alcohol goes, how it gets from place to place, and what each part of your body does to it.

The chart may look confusing, but your average goldfish can probably help explain it to you if you need help. Read on!

OXIDATION CHART

1. **Mouth.** Alcohol is drunk.
2. **Stomach.** Alcohol goes right into the stomach. A little of the alcohol goes through the wall of the stomach and into the bloodstream. But most of the alcohol goes down into the *small intestine.*
3. **Small intestine.** Alcohol goes from the stomach into the small intestine. Most of the alcohol then goes through the walls of the intestine and into the *bloodstream.*
4. **Bloodstream.** The bloodstream then carries the alcohol to *all* parts of the body, such as the brain, heart, and *liver.*
5. **Liver.** As the bloodstream carries the alcohol around the body, it carries it through the liver, too. The liver changes the alcohol to water, carbon dioxide, and energy. This process is called *oxidation.* The liver can oxidize (change into water, carbon dioxide, and energy) only about one-half ounce of alcohol an hour. This means that until the liver has time to oxidize all of the alcohol, the alcohol *keeps on* passing through all parts of the body, including the *brain.*
6. **Brain.** Alcohol goes to the brain almost as soon as it is drunk. The bloodstream carries it there. Alcohol keeps passing through the brain until the liver has had time to change (oxidize) all the alcohol into carbon dioxide, water and energy.

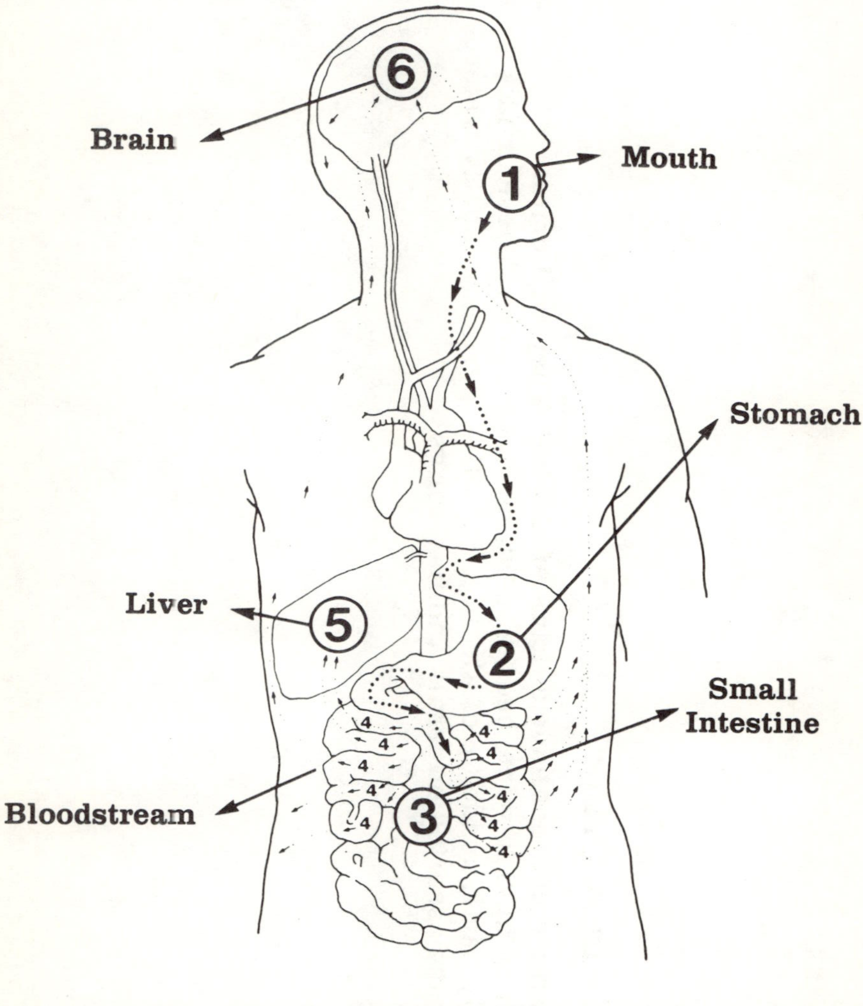

As you can see from this chart, when someone has a drink, the alcohol goes to and continues to pass through his or her brain. But how a drinker *feels* as the alcohol keeps on passing through the brain depends partly on *how many drinks* he or she takes.

(Diagram by Linda W. Clement)

What's In A Drink?

People don't just have a drink of alcohol! They will drink alcohol by having wine, beer, gin, whiskey, and so on. These drinks are only partly made up of alcohol. The other parts are mostly water with some assorted minerals and flavorings.

Let's examine these three types of drinks in terms of alcohol, and compare them.

- Take beer for example: Most beers contain 4-6% alcohol.
- Wines have a bit more alcohol than beer — usually between 12% and 20%. Wines also have fruit juice and minerals and other chemicals in them, but mostly water.
- The greatest amounts of alcohol are found in spirits, or hard liquor. These beverages (such as whiskey, rum, brandy, gin, etc.) are usually close to 50% alcohol!

A 5-ounce wine glass has ½ ounce of alcohol.

A 12-ounce can of beer contains ½ ounce of alcohol.

A shot (1½ ounces) of liquor has ½ ounce of alcohol.

Look Again!

You can see from the picture on page 80 that it doesn't matter whether people drink **a can of beer, a glass of wine, or a shot of liquor — they all contain the same amount of alcohol.** The quantity of liquid is obviously different, but the actual amount of alcohol is the same.

Mixed Drniks (?)

Many people seem to think that a **mixed drink** (drink made with hard liquor plus a mixer such as ginger ale, water, or fruit juice) is stronger (has more alcohol) than a glass of wine or a can of beer. Wrong!!!

A mixed drink made with **only one shot of liquor** has the same amount of alcohol as a can of beer or a glass of wine.
However ... people mix their drinks differently.

Question

. . . See if you can explain why many of the **mixed drinks** people make very often **do have much more alcohol** in them than a can of beer or a glass of wine. (Are you thinking? Good! Now Write!)

"I think . . . ____

____

____

____

Answer

Many mixed drinks contain more alcohol because people put more than one shot of liquor in their drinks. Sometimes these drinks have as much as two or more shots of liquor in them. Some people don't measure how much they put in. It is for these reasons that many mixed drinks have so much more alcohol than wine or beer.

In addition, cocktails such as Martinis and Manhattans are made by combining wine and hard liquor. As a result of this combination, these cocktails often have two or even three times as much alcohol as a glass of wine or a can of beer.

Remember: After all is said and done, it is the **amount of alcohol** which you consume that makes the difference.

Activity No. 21, What's Your Opinion?

Discuss these questions in class, with a friend or friends, at home, or with your sister's pet warthog.

1. What is there about alcohol that makes it a drug?
2. How do T.V. commercials for beers and wines try to trick you into thinking you ought to drink?
3. Do people need to drink?
4. What's the difference between good drinking and bad drinking?
5. When you have problems, what are alternative ways of dealing with them — other than using drugs?
6. How else, besides using drugs, can you get high? (Remember: Alcohol is a drug.)

Alcohol A Drug??

Were you surprised to see alcohol called a drug? Thought you might be. Don't believe it? Ask your doctor! Better yet, have your doctor buy one of these books for himself (or herself).

So far you've seen how alcohol travels through the body and how to compare different drinks and how much alcohol they each have.

- What — you ask — can happen to people who drink?
- Well — we say — let's look at **what alcohol can do to and for people.**

To Begin With . .

Small or **moderate** (there's a word to look up) amounts of alcohol can have a wide variety of effects on people. Depending on many things, a drink or two might . . .

. . . appear to have no effect at all on a person.

A drink or two might . . .

. . . make a person feel tired or

. . . make it easier for some people to have a good time.

A drink or two might also . . .

. . . cause people to feel more energetic or

. . . make it more difficult to think clearly.

90 **Too much alcohol also may have a variety of effects.** Too much alcohol might . . .

. . . cause some people to be very loud and silly acting

or

. . . cause others to become very unhappy or mean acting.

Too much alcohol might . . .

. . . cause people to stumble and become clutzy

or

. . . cause others to lose their ability to concentrate on what they're saying or doing.

Too much alcohol might also . . .

. . . cause people to **say things they'll regret** or

. . . cause others to do things they'll regret later.

Question

So, it is now obvious that the drug alcohol has the same effect on everyone — it **acts as a stimulant** — right? _________ (Don't tell me you don't know what stimulant is — well that's O.K. — you can easily look it up in your trusty glossary or you could even ask someone — like your teacher, nurse, or fairy godmother — anyhow we're not going to tell you everything in this little book — we're not nuts!)

Answer — Wrongo!!!

There is nothing stimulating about alcohol. In fact, alcohol acts as a total depressant, slowing down the body's central nervous system. And that system only allows you to think, act, react, and other little goodies that you might want to be able to do.

Question

Why does alcohol do different things to different people? Why do some people get sleepy and others get talkative after drinking? Why do some people become mean and others more pleasant?

Answer

One reason people act and feel differently is due to how much alcohol they drink.

A person who has had five or six drinks is probably going to feel (and act) differently from a person who has had just one.

But not always . . . because . . .

Here's Why . . .

If one person has just one beer in one hour, and another takes four or five hours to drink five beers, the alcohol may have just about the same overall effect on both of them. There are **a number of other important factors** which play a role in how a person behaves and feels after he or she drinks.

Pay attention. This is going to be tricky!

How a Person Behaves and Feels After He or She Drinks Also Depends On . . .

1. How quickly they drink
2. How much the drinker weighs
3. Drinking experience
4. Food in the drinker's stomach
5. One's feeling about alcohol
6. The drinker's mood
7. Where someone drinks

These will be discussed and explained on the next few pages. Pay attention so you'll be able to explain them to your teacher.

Question

Your liver changes (oxidizes) alcohol into carbon dioxide, water and energy. It can oxidize a drink (one-half ounce of alcohol) in . . .

A. One day

B. One hour

C. One-half hour

D. One week

Having trouble with this one? Why not peek back at your basic oxidation chart — easily found on pages 76-77.

Answer

B you say?

Right you are wizard! And we don't care if you did look back. The **liver can oxidize one-half ounce of alcohol in about one hour.**

Question

Can you make the connection?

If one person drinks five beers in five hours, his/her liver has about as much time to process (oxidize) the alcohol as in the case of another person who has one beer in . . .

A. A week

B. An hour

C. Thirty minutes

D. A minute

Answer

Even *you* got the right answer! It's **B** — sure — one hour.

Because in both cases not much alcohol stays in the bloodstream, since the liver can process it easily at those rates.

So, it's not only **how much a person drinks that is important, it is also how quickly!** The fact is, the faster a person drinks, the greater is the amount of alcohol that will remain in his/her brain.

In this case, drinking is like driving — slow down and live!

Question

Who would probably feel the effects of drinking 3 beers in one hour most strongly? (Circle one)

A. A 175 pound man

B. A 130 pound man

C. A 400 pound carp (he drinks like a fish!)

Why? ____

____

____

Answer

B. The 130 pound man would be affected more strongly than a larger person who drank the same amount in the same time.

Why? The larger person has more blood and water in his/her body. These fluids will act to dilute (weaken) the strength of the alcohol in the person's bloodsteam.

Sooo . . .

You can see that body weight is an important factor in how alcohol affects a person.

We've looked at . . .

- How much a person drinks
- How quickly a person drinks
- Body weight

Now let's look at some other important factors showing how alcohol affects a person.

(Are you still with us?)

Another Factor is the Presence of Food in the Drinker's Stomach.

If a person drinks while eating (or shortly after eating), the food in the stomach slows down the rate that alcohol gets into the small intestine. Remember, most alcohol (about 85%) gets into the bloodstream and then to the brain from the small intestine.

Sooo . . . **Food in the stomach will slow down the effects of alcohol.**

Another Factor is Drinking Experience.

People who have been drinking alcohol for a number of years should have learned what alcohol does to them. They may have learned to be careful about what they do and say while drinking. (If they don't drink too much.)

A bad part of this is that with long use of alcohol may come **tolerance.** This means that the body gets used to alcohol, and that the drinker may need more alcohol to get the same kick or high.

Sooo . . .

You've seen how **body size, experience, food, speed,** and **quantity** all play a role in how alcohol affects people, but did you know that how a person views alcohol is also important?

That's right, what a drinker things and feels — their **expectations** — about alcohol can also make a tremendous difference.

In Fact . . .

Expectations alone can really produce an effect.

For example, as an experiment to prove this, some college students were served several drinks each. They thought the drinks were alcoholic, but they were not. They got high on them. Since these students **expected** to get somewhat drunk, they did—yep—drunk without alcohol—how about that!

Moody?

The **mood that someone is in while drinking is another influence on how alcohol may affect the person.** A person in a good or happy mood may get very happy or friendly. A person who is sad may feel very unhappy while drinking. Other moods such as being angry or nervous may also affect the person's behavior while drinking.

Where and When

It might seem odd, but **where a person drinks** and in what circumstances (look it up and you'll be smarter!) can also be important to the way alcohol affects a person. For example, someone drinking with others may feel very happy, but drinking alone at home may cause the same person to feel unhappy or lonely.

Question

You've just read about many reasons that drinking causes people to behave differently. The effects of alcohol depend on several factors — remember? — How many can you list?

1. ______________________________________

2. ______________________________________

3. ______________________________________

4. ______________________________________

5. ______________________________________

6. ______________________________________

7. ______________________________________

8. ______________________________________

Answer

The effects of alcohol depend on:

- Amount consumed
- Speed of drinking
- Drinker's weight
- Drinking experience
- Food in the drinker's stomach
- Expectations — one's feelings about alcohol
- Drinker's mood
- Where one drinks

Thinking About Drinking

Sooo — you really can't say "drinking makes you feel this" or "alcohol does this to you," because often these kinds of statements are wrong! **Unless we consider all the factors** we've listed, we really can't accurately state what alcohol will do to ourselves.

Of course, the ads on television, never really deal with this stuff. They just try to make it inviting so they can make lots of money!

Also . . .

This means that it is equally difficult to know how alcohol will act on others. It takes many years of experience with alcohol before you can predict how you will probably act or feel. After many years people learn what happens to them when they drink (usually).

Our guess is . . . that you have learned a lot about alcohol from this part of the book. Hopefully, that means you won't let someone else talk you into doing something really stupid!

Activity No. 864, Finish the Sentence

Copy and complete each sentence. Discuss your ideas in class or at home.

1. "Two people who drink the same amount ..."
2. "Drinking ..."
3. "Drinkers ..."
4. "Good things about alcohol ..."
5. "Alcoholic people are ..."
6. "Not everyone ..."
7. "The drug, alcohol, is ..."
8. "The way to deal with alcoholics is ..."

Activity No. 627, Game Time

Get with two or three other kids (because lamp shades are boring to work with) and design a board game (like Monopoly or Sorry) about alcohol. Your kind, generous teacher may supply the materials if you ask nicely. Make sure to include a list of rules.

Plan a class game day with time to show and play each group's game. Maybe your class could invite another class to play your games.

FIRST STEP!
FIRST WORD!
FIRST KISS!
FIRST DRINK?

Who Drinks and Who Doesn't

By what age do you think most Americans have had their first drink? Go ahead . . . think about it . . . we'll wait . . . well . . . what do you think? The answer is that most have had their first drink in elementary or junior high school. Is that true for you and your friends? Should it be? (Don't rush out and start if you haven't! We're trying to learn to be responsible, remember?)

This means that a lot of **kids around your age** have had that **first drink** by now, usually at home **with their parents.**

It doesn't mean that most of the kids your age are out "drinking" every night and getting drunk.

Thought Question

Most kids who drink say that they like it. What do you think they enjoy about drinking?

"I think ... ______________________________

____

____

____

Discuss your ideas with another person.

Do you think that those who drink give their *real* reasons? Can you think of others?

"I think ... ______________________________

____

____

Kids Who Drink

Most kids in junior high school who drink do so only once in a while and usually drink beer or wine.

But many kids who drink, or who are thinking about starting, wonder what drinking might do to them. Some are afraid of how alcohol might affect them. They don't know if it will hurt them. They might be afraid that if they start drinking they might not be able to ever stop.

Thought Question

If you are wondering about drinking and may be a little bit afraid, how can you learn more about alcohol in ways that aren't dangerous?

"I think ... ____

____

____

____

Discuss this with another person (or with an intelligent bologna sandwich).

Ask Yourself . . .

Another question you might ask yourself is whether there are more kids with problems because of drinking too much or whether there are more kids with problems because of using other drugs like PCP, Pot, Speed, or Coke.

Think about this — think about it and how it applies to you and your friends.

Notice that a person can have problems with alcohol, just as they can have problems with other drugs.

TRUE OR FALSE?

The really serious problem in America today is drug abuse.

True or False? ____________________

True!

Drug abuse is a really serious problem and **the number one drug abused is alcohol.** Over 9,000,000 Americans have drinking problems.

Thought Question

If more kids have drinking problems than problems with other drugs, why do so many adults worry more about the other drugs than about alcohol?

"I think ... ____

____

____

____

Discuss your answer with a friend (or a cucumber that wants to converse).

What do your parents think? Well, ask them!

Why Do Many Adults Worry Less About Alcohol Than About Other Drugs?

- Maybe they don't know that **alcohol is a drug.** (It is, you know. It's a depressant, a downer.)
- Maybe they feel that alcohol is an acceptable drug to abuse, while other drugs are unacceptable.
- Maybe they don't have as much common sense as a bowl of pickle ice-cream! Who knows?

What do you think?

"I think ... ______________________________

____

____

Prevention

We've all heard about prevention. It means stopping trouble before it starts. Vaccines prevent illness; we get dental checkups and use fluoride toothpaste to prevent cavities; we practice fire safety. Prevention works — especially for alcohol abuse problems.

For you and your friends, **prevention means knowing what alcohol can do to you and for you and then deciding whether or not to use it.**

Activity No. 17, "Dear Abby"

Write an answer to the following Dear Abby letter. (Use your decision-making skills from Chapter 1 to help you.) Write your answer on a sheet of your own paper (or grovel and beg one from your teacher). Share your answers in class.

Dear Abby,

Last week my three friends and I went downtown. We met some older kids who had beer in their car. They gave a six-pack to one of my friends who wanted to "see what it's like." My friends thought this was great and we all went to the park to drink. I refused to drink because I think I'm too young. (I'm 12), and because I don't want the hassle of getting caught by my folks and punished. Now my "friends" are making life miserable for me. They call me a "drip" and a "chicken" and make fun of me. I *do* want them for friends (they *really are good kids),* but I'm not going to take any more from them. What can I do?

Sincerely,
Confused

Speaking of Prevention . . .

What is the best cure for a hangover? (look up hangover in the **GLOSSARY**.)

"I think ... ____

____

____

____

____

Answer

Everyone has a favorite cure, and they all have one thing in common—they don't work. The only cure is time: the **time it takes to get rid of all the alcohol and its effects**. A better cure is prevention—if a person doesn't drink, or doesn't drink too much, he/she won't get a hangover.

Why Do Kids Drink (or not drink)?

There are many reasons why kids make the decisions they do about drinking. We're going to list a few and talk about them. Maybe you will be able to think of more reasons as we go along. If so, add them to our list.

- Many kids drink because it's part of their family life to have wine at dinner or at a social occasion like a holiday or wedding Their parents may give them wine or a taste of beer at dinner or a party.

- Many young people drink in order to feel big or grown-up.

Some Other Reasons . . .

- Some kids drink because they have a drinking problem — **alcoholism.** These kids come from all walks of life — rich or poor, black or white, girls or boys.

- Many kids are pressured to drink by other kids (this happens to adults, too). This is called **peer pressure**, and it's tough to resist. Many of us don't like to be different, or be a chicken, or a party pooper, no matter what our age.

Let's talk more about peer pressure. Try the activity on the next page.

TRUE OR FALSE?

Peer pressure can persuade us to act or not act against our own wishes. This is usually not as good as making our own decisions.

True or False? ____________________

TRUE!

Often we allow others to make decisions for us that we later have to accept responsibility for. As long as **you are held responsible for a decision,** shouldn't *you* be the one who makes it (using the methods from Chapter 1, of course)?

Activity No. 43-Y, "Good and Bad" Reasons

Here are some other reasons kids give for why they drink:

- "It relaxes me."
- "It helps me have a good time."
- "It tastes good."
- "I'm curious about what it's like."
- "My friends do it."
- "It makes me like myself better."
- "It helps me forget my problems."
- "My parents drink."
- "My parents told me not to drink."

Look at this list. Add to it if you can. **Circle** the reasons that you feel are good reasons. Put an **X** in front of the reasons you feel are bad.

How did you decide what's good or bad? Do you think adults drink for any of these same reasons?

Some People Who Don't Drink Have Other Reasons . . .

For some it is against the beliefs of their family, friends, or religion to use alcohol. How do you feel about these people and these beliefs?

"I think ... ____

____

____

Thought Question

Why do you think that many people—kids and adults—**don't drink?**

"I think ... ________________

____

____

____

____

____

____

____

Some Possible Answers

Between 20 and 30 million Americans never or hardly ever drink alcohol. Here are some reasons why:

- They may not be interested in it.
- They don't feel they need it to feel good or to be grown-up.
- They're happy the way they are.
- They have other ways of relaxing and having fun.
- They don't drink for religious reasons.
- They don't like to use any drugs, including alcohol.

> Which of these reasons do you feel are good and which are bad? **Circle** the good and put an **X** in front of the bad ones. Then survey some other people and get their opinions.

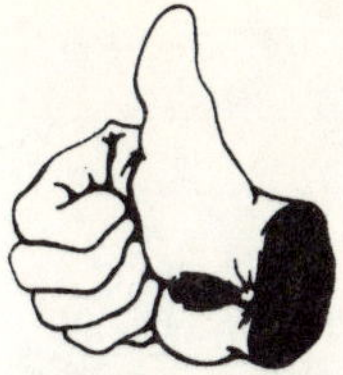

Activity No. 714, More Dear Abby

Make up Dear Abby problems of your own and exchange them in class for Abby's advice.

Dear Abby,

____

____

____

____

____

____

____

____

Signed,

What do kids know and think about drinking?

Adults and kids have many different ideas and beliefs about alcohol and drinking. As we read in Chapter 2, **much of what we think is wrong,** and it is this wrong information which can contribute to problems with alcohol.

Try the activity on the next page (if you don't you'll turn into a pumpkin).

Activity No. 2, Outguess the High-School Kids

The following statements were given to high school students. More than half of the students thought that all these statements were **true**. What do you think? Put an **X** in the box of your choice. Answers are on the next page (but don't peek or your brain will turn into oatmeal!).

1. It's pretty easy to tell if a person is drunk.

   TRUE ☐ FALSE ☐

2. A small person will usually get drunk faster than a large person.

   TRUE ☐ FALSE ☐

3. A shot of whiskey is stronger (has more alcohol) than a glass of wine.

   TRUE ☐ FALSE ☐

4. Mixing different types of drinks can increase the effects of alcohol.

   TRUE ☐ FALSE ☐

5. The caffeine in strong black coffee can help a person sober up.

   TRUE ☐ FALSE ☐

Answers

1. **FALSE** — As we saw in Chapter 3, people show the effects of alcohol in different ways.
2. **TRUE** — A larger person has more body fluid to dilute (look that up) the alcohol and slow down its effects.
3. **FALSE** — Remember Chapter 2? Of course you do!
4. **FALSE** — It's the **amount** of alcohol, not its form that makes the difference.
5. **FALSE** — The ONLY cure for being drunk is time. It takes **time** for the body to burn up the alcohol. Remember, the liver is the only part of the body that can do this — slowly.

How did you do on this quiz? If you got them *all* right, then you did better than most high school students *and* most adults. (If you didn't get *any* right then you need to try reading this book with your eyes open.)

CHAPTER 5

DRINKING PROBLEMS

"Ya gotta hand it to Joe.
He really can hold his liquor."

What is a drinking problem?

Well, it depends on how you look at it. Some people feel that any drinking at all is too much. Others feel that it is okay to drink some, but they have a certain limit (like 2 or 3 cocktails each night) that they feel is too much. We think that what is too much is a **decision that you must make.**

This portion of our book will help you to understand some of the problems that drinking has caused for individuals, families, and our country as a whole.

Using Alcohol

Let's look at three different ways that people use (or don't use) alcohol.

- First, some people do **no drinking** at all. They are called **abstainers.** Obviously, they do not have a drinking problem.
- Second, some people are called **social drinkers.** They usually don't drink too much. They usually drink in social situations with other people. They drink to relax or celebrate, *not* to get drunk. Their drinking probably doesn't cause any problems. This group has the largest number in it, and the line between this type of drinking and the type described on the next page can become a fine one.

And . . .

- Finally, **people who drink too much** and whose drinking causes trouble for themselves and/or others are called **problem drinkers**, or **alcoholics**. There are **more than 9 million Americans in this group.**

Instant Quiz

Draw lines from each type of person to match his/her behavior toward alcohol.

Social Drinker	Does not drink!
Problem Drinker (Alcoholic)	Drinks for relaxation and enjoyment; no problems with alcohol.
Abstainer	Drinks too much!

Don't mess this up, 'cause it's really easy (unless you have been at the South Pole for the last 10 years).

Answers

Social drinker	Does not drink
Problem drinker	Drinks for relaxation and enjoyment; no problems with alcohol.
Abstainer	Drinks too much!

We just knew you would get these all correct! We're so proud of you!

Thought Questions

What do you think some **advantages** of being an abstainer might be?

"I think ... ____

____

____

What do you think some **disadvantages** of abstaining might be?

"I think ... ____

____

Discuss your ideas in class or in small groups (or with 3 of your favorite super-heroes).

Think About This

There are many advantages of being an abstainer or non-drinker, but probably the best advantage is that you will always have the choice.

". . . .**To drink or not to drink**"—think about it!

In this next part of the chapter, we are going to look at problem drinkers — alcoholics. We'll look at who they are and what kinds of problems they have.

TRUE OR FALSE?

People with drinking problems hurt only themselves.
True or False? ____________________

False (We knew we couldn't fool you!)
Problem drinkers hurt themselves, their families, friends, employers, co-workers, strangers on the highways—maybe even you.

Who Are These Problem Drinkers?

They are called **alcoholics**, and there are more than 10 million of them. They suffer from a disease called **alcoholism**. They are having problems with the drug called alcohol. They are probably hooked on alcohol—physically or emotionally.

How do we know a person is a problem drinker? Study the next few pages for some examples of persons who are problem drinkers.

1. A person who needs several drinks first thing in the morning or to get to sleep at night.

2. **A person who can't work without being high or drunk.**

3. Anybody who drives a car after drinking too much.

Question

What fraction of fatal highway accidents do you think involve drinking?

A. 1/3　　B. 1/2　　C. 9/5

Answer

B. At least 1/2 of highway deaths involve drinking. (If you picked C, you better hide from your math teacher!)

By the way, did you know that a person who is convicted of **driving while intoxicated (DWI)** is in very serious trouble? A good extra credit project would be to investigate the laws concerning drinking and driving in your county and state.

Now, let's look at some more problem drinkers.

4. People who drink and then get into fights or arguments.

5. Someone who **needs** alcohol before meeting people or going to places where he or she will be with other people.

6. Any person whose drinking is causing a health problem.

Some other ways that people with drinking problems can be identified include:

7. They might have **blackouts**—loss of memory of what they do while drinking.
8. Sometimes they might go on a **bender**—a long drinking spree of non-stop drinking.
9. They might make a lot of excuses for their drinking and deny that they have a problem.
10. They might hide alcohol and drink secretly.
11. They may need more and more alcohol to get high or drunk. This is called tolerance.
12. They may reach the point where they **get sick if they don't drink.**

Activity No. 1492, Draw a Problem

On a large piece of paper, illustrate one of the ways just listed that could be a **symptom of a drinking problem** (or use a different one that you can think of).

Color your picture neatly. (Stay inside the lines or you will find liquified crayon in your milk at lunch time.) Display class pictures on a bulletin board.

Question

We gave you **12 ways that people with drinking problems may behave.** How many can you remember? List them below or on a separate piece of paper, and then look back and fill in the rest.

1. **7.**

2. **8.**

3. **9.**

4. **10.**

5. **11.**

6. **12.**

SCORING:

11-12 Excellent
8-10 Good
6-7 Fair
2-5 Poor
0-1 El Stinko!

We've told you some ways that you can identify drinking problems. Here are some ways that you *can't*.

1. You can't assume that all alcoholics are drunken, skid row bums! Actually, *most problem drinkers seem to be living normal lives. They work, marry, have kids . . .* but they also drink too much.

2. You can't assume that most alcoholics are poor (or black, or young, or old, or men, or women, or ..., or ..., or ...). In fact, **there is no general alcoholic type.** Rather, alcoholics come from *all* groups, ages, races, jobs, sexes, etc., with this in common — they are having problems because of the drug, alcohol.

3. You can't assume that you don't know any alcoholics. **Maybe you just don't realize that you know some alcoholics.** Remember they come from all walks of life. They don't seem different. They usually try to hide their illness (and won't admit it). Some of your best friends may have drinking problems.

Question

Which of these is a more realistic view of alcohol and drugs?

A. Taking other drugs is worse than having a problem with alcohol.

B. If a person has a drug problem, it could be with alcohol or any other drug. It's still a **big problem.**

Answer

B. Alcohol or any other drug problem is serious. (In fact, alcohol abuse is the biggest drug problem among young people!)

Question

Is it possible to have a drug problem with more than one kind of drug?

YES or NO? ____________________ (Use your head, Fred!)

Answer

It sure is!

Unfortunately, many people have problems combining drugs, including alcohol. This creates even more serious problems!

Can Alcoholics or Problem Drinkers Be Helped?

It is hard to explain why the number of men and women (and kids) who have drinking problems is so high in this country. One thing is for sure though, most (probably all) people who have drinking problems **can get help** to either decrease their drinking or else to stop drinking entirely.

It was once thought that people who were alcoholics could be helped by throwing them in jail!

This, of course, is ridiculous! Alcoholism is recognized as a serious illness. People who are sick with other diseases aren't put behind bars. **There are treatments for alcoholism** — just as there are treatments for most illnesses.

Sometimes, frightening or tragic events will cause alcoholics to stop drinking. They might be involved in a serious accident. Their wives, or husbands, or children, might decide to leave them finally. They might develop a serious health problem. Some problem drinkers might just outgrow their problem—and stop (or slow down) drinking as they get older.

But—problem drinkers have a disease called alcoholism. Until they get help for themselves, they will continue to drink **too much.**

HELP!

Problem drinkers can be helped. The most successful treatments involve their talking about their problems. This can be done with many people. It could be a friend or a relative, but often these people lack the training to be most effective.

You would not, for example, take your little brother to the T.V. repairman to get his teeth cleaned — or would you? Well — hopefully you wouldn't.

People Who Need People ...

By the same token, problem drinkers need people with special training and education to properly help them. There are many people available to help.

Young people with drinking problems can get help from many sources. Guidance counselors, social workers, doctors, school nurse-teachers, and others that you know and respect can help young people with problems. And if they can't, they can surely tell the problem drinkers where to go to get help.

Alcoholics Anonymous

All over the world there are Alcoholics Anonymous (AA) groups. AA provides help by allowing and encouraging problem drinkers to talk to recovering alcoholics. Every member of AA is a recovering alcoholic — they no longer drink at all. A huge number of **alcoholics have been greatly helped by joining Alcoholics Anonymous.**

Find the location of the Alcoholics Anonymous branch nearest you. Write its address and phone number here:

____

____

Activity No. 93, Local Help

Find a partner who you want to work with (or pay someone to help you), and find as many local agencies as you can who have trained counselors who will work to help people with drinking problems. List them here:

NAME	ADDRESS	PHONE
1.		
2.		
3.		

(Use more paper if necessary)

Visit, call, or write one or more of these agencies. You might want to report to your class on your contacts — or compare notes on the above list — or invite them to speak to your class — or — or — or ...

TRUE OR FALSE?

To be considered as a "recovering alcoholic" you must be someone who no longer drinks alcohol.

True of False? ____________________

True! (Tricky question—huh?)

Yep—in order for most people to deal with the disease called alcoholism, they must completely stop their use of the drug called alcohol.

How Do You Live With An Alcoholic?

There are groups similar to Alcoholics Anonymous that help people related to alcoholics. **Alateen** uses the AA model of counseling and serves teenagers with alcoholic parents. **Al-Anon** serves husbands or wives of alcoholics. In both these groups there are usually weekly sessions to talk about ways for the members to help the alcoholic in their family — and how best to live with them. They also share experiences and methods of helping themselves live in their situations.

Help Wanted

There are lots of places where problem drinkers can get help—once they **admit** they have a problem—and once **they decide that they want help.**

If you know anyone who has a problem with the drug, alcohol, try and get them to seek help. Try to get them to contact Alcoholics Anonymous or one of the other agencies you listed on page 175.

Help is available — for the asking.

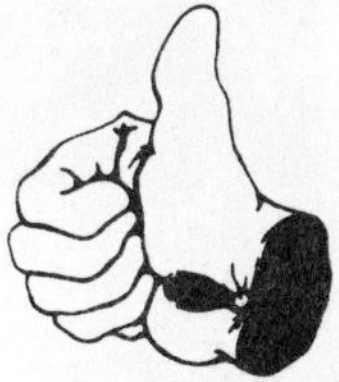

Activity No. 321A, Statements

Below are five commonly heard statements relating to alcohol. Pick one (or more) of them and **write down your feelings and thoughts about them.** Find someone in class to discuss them with. Discuss them all with your friends or class. Discuss them with your pet hippopotomas. Talk them over with yourself in front of a mirror or in the shower.

- "Refusing a drink is impolite."
- "It's not nice to tell friends that they're drinking too much."
- "I can quit drinking anytime."
- "Alcoholism isn't a sickness, just a state of mind."
- "Not me, I'll never have a drinking problem."

Alcohol Crossword Puzzle

If you want to test how much you know about alcohol, try doing this crossword puzzle. You can do it alone or with two or three classmates. (Answers to the puzzle are on page 182 — but don't peek!).

Across

(1) Some people get ______ after drinking alcohol.

(6) Alcohol doesn't have such a strong effect when people have some ______ in their stomach.

(8) An alcoholic drink made from grapes.

(11) If someone who is drunk wants to drive you someplace, you can agree or ______ (rhymes with agree).

(14) Physical education (abbreviation)

(15) Most wines have either a red or yellow ______.

(16) Some people think drinking is dull; others think it's ______.

(18) A type of hard liquor.

(19) If you played hockey while you were drunk, you would probably ______ on the ice many times.

(21) Another word for "I."

(22) As far as we know, one or two drinks a day has ______ bad effects on a healthy person.

(24) You may eat it for breakfast, but it is also what whiskey is made from.

(25) He sang "Hound Dog," "Love Me Tender," and "Jailhouse Rock."

(26) If someone drinks too much, he or she may pass ______ .

(27) When someone drinks alcohol, it travels by the bloodstream from the small intestine ______ the liver.

(28) A huge company that makes telephones and sends telegrams.

(30) The word "salty," but change the 'y' to another vowel.

(32) Beer is often sold in a ______ pack.

(33) An urgent request; a type of begging.

(34) Abbreviation for the word "year."

Down

(1) "I'll ______ a bottle of French wine for three bottles of German beer. Is it a deal?"

(2) Some people, after they've had a few drinks, start to feed you a ______ about all the great things they say they've done.

(3) Player (or position) on a football team.

(4) The word "ever" spelled with one of its letters missing.

(5) A type of evergreen tree. (Rhymes with "you.")

(6) Drunk drivers cause about half of the ______ thousand auto deaths which take place every year.

(7) People who are on a ______ shouldn't drink too much alcohol because it has too many calories.

(10) The word "even" with one letter missing.

(12) Alcoholics often have to ______ about why they took a drink.

(13) The 5th and 14th letters of the alphabet.

(16) If your mother or father found you drunk, would she or he have a ______ ?

(17) Drinking too much alcohol may ______ your stomach.

(18) Alcohol helps many people rest and ______ after a nervous day. (Synonym for sleep.)

(19) There are ice cream ______ and Scotch and ______ .

(20) Sixth note of the musical scale.

(21) Name for a player on a New York baseball team.

(22) Some people who drink too much behave silly and ______ , as if they were crazy.

(23) Relative of a beaver.

(26) A liquid that helps a car run smoothly.

(31) A group that helps alcoholics. (Initials).

Answers to crossword puzzle

1 S	2 L	3 E	4 E	P	5 Y		6 F	O	O	7 D
8 W	I	N	E		E		I			I
9 A	N	D	R	10 E	W		11 F	12 L	13 E	E
14 P	E			E			15 T	I	N	T
		16 F	17 U	N		18 R	Y	E		
19 S	20 L	I	P		21 M	E			22 N	23 O
24 O	A	T	S		25 E	P		26 O	U	T
D			E		27 T	O		28 I	T	T
29 A			T			30 S	31 A	L	T	E
32 S	I	X		33 P	L	E	A		34 Y	R

CHAPTER 6

IT'S UP TO YOU!

Victim or Chooser?

You probably remember (sure you do!) that at the beginning of this little book we raised this question:

Do I have control over my life? (Am I a **victim** or a **chooser**?)

Let's think about this question . . .

We hope that you have noticed that we haven't preached at you in this book, and we haven't told you whether you should or should not drink. (At least we hope that you've noticed that.)

PS-E!

One of the most powerful influences on your life (thoughts, attitudes, even actions), is PS-E. These letters stand for **positive self-expectation.**

People who expect something positive in their lives take control of their lives. They set goals, and try to obtain those goals. This is very important in decision-making.

As you develop **positive self-expectation** and begin making your own decisions—and being responsible for those decisions—you will then be taking control of your own life.

What Have We Done Then?

We have tried to give you some **facts about alcohol and drinking.** We have tried to help you to examine your own values and to get to know yourself a little better.

Most importantly, we have tried to help you to learn a process, a method that you can use to help you to make decisions, especially *big* decisions like **whether or not to drink alcohol.**

Because, you see for *you* to have control over your life, **it's important that you make responsible decisions about your life.** *You* (and only you) must be willing to accept the responsibility, for what *you* decide. Responsibility — that's the key. Think about it.

It's your life! Work hard with it! Talk to others about it! Expect some ups and downs! And maybe you too will **GET HIGH ON LIFE!**

Activity No. 73, Posters, Pamphlets, and Stuff

Collect some information about alcohol. Use one (or more) of these ideas. (Or think of some ways on your own, smartie.)

1. Make a scrapbook of newspaper clippings (or a collage, or bulletin board).
2. Visit one of the agencies you found in Chapter 5, **Drinking Problems.** Bring posters, pamphlets, booklets, etc. to class.
3. Write for free materials:

National Clearinghouse for Alcohol Information
Box 2345
Rockville, Maryland 28852

If you enjoyed reading **KIDS AND ALCOHOL** (and we're certain that you did), you are sure to enjoy the other two books in the **Get High on Life** series . . .

KIDS AND SMOKING — you and Bumper will learn the facts about using tobacco.

KIDS AND DRUGS — journey with Bumper as he explores the use and abuse of drugs.

Both books will **help you learn how to make decisions** and **take more control of your own life.**

GLOSSARY

Here are the meanings of many of the terms used in the **study of alcohol.**

Absorption — The process by which alcohol gets into the bloodstream from the stomach and small intestine.

Abstainer — One who does not drink alcohol.

Al-Anon — Organization of wives and husbands of alcoholics. It helps members in living with their alcoholic spouses.

Alateen — Organization for teenagers who have an alcoholic parent. Members get help in living with an alcoholic mother or father.

Alcohol — A colorless liquid found in beer, wine, or spirits which affects the central nervous system.

Alcoholic — A person who suffers from an illness called alcoholism; a problem drinker.

Alcoholics Anonymous (AA) — An organization of recovering alcoholics. Members help each other to live without alcohol.

Alcoholism — A disease where a person's body and mind need alcohol, the alcoholic is dependent on the drug, alcohol.

Bender — A long period of drinking and drunkenness; like being drunk two or three days or more.

Blackout — A loss of memory of what one did or said while drunk.

Dependent — A condition where a person's body and/or mind needs a drug.

Depressant — Often called a downer, a drug which slows down the working of the body's central nervous system.

Dilute — To make something weaker by adding a liquid to it.

Distillation — The process of making hard liquor. A liquid containing alcohol is heated to turn the alcohol into gas. This gas is then cooled and becomes pure liquid alcohol.

Drug — Any substance (other than food) which affects the way the mind or body works. Drugs can be inhaled, absorbed through the skin, swallowed or injected into the bloodstream.

Drunk — The way a person feels and acts when under the influence of alcohol. A drunk, or intoxicated person usually has lost control of his or her thoughts and actions.

Drunk and Disorderly — A situation where a person is drunk and acting up (yelling, fighting, etc.) in public. This is against the law in most states.

DWI - Driving While Intoxicated, a serious crime in most states.

Ethyl Alcohol — The form of alcohol which is in beer, wine and spirits. It is the only kind of alcohol which is safe to drink.

Fermentation — The action of yeast on the sugar in fruit juices or cereal to produce alcohol.

Hangover — A sick feeling (headache, upset stomach) which people can get several hours after having been drunk or high. This happens after the alcohol has left the body and the drinker is sober.

High — A state of feeling when alcohol has started to make a person feel good, but not to the point where the person has lost control over words and actions.

Intestine — Organ through which food and liquids pass after leaving the stomach. Alcohol passes into the bloodstream from the small intestine.

Kidneys — Organs which remove liquid wastes from the bloodstream.

Legal Drinking Age — The age, in most states, at which a person may purchase or be served alcohol in liquor stores, bars, and restaurants.

Liver — The only organ in the body which can oxidize (change) alcohol into carbon dioxide and water.

Lungs — Organs where oxygen enters the bloodstream and carbon dioxide is removed.

Methyl Alcohol — A *poisonous* form of alcohol used in industry in anti-freeze, fuels, and paint thinner; processed from wood and is sometimes called wood alcohol.

Minor — A person who is not legally an adult. The age at which a person is legally an adult varies from state to state. (See legal drinking age.)

Oxidation — The process where the liver adds oxygen to alcohol to produce carbon dioxide and water.

Oxygen — Gas inhaled by the lungs and carried throughout the body in the bloodstream.

Peer — A person of about the same age and position in life as you.

Peer Pressure — When people who are your peers (but don't have authority over you) try to push you into doing, or not doing, something.

Problem Drinker — An alcoholic whose drinking causes problems for him/herself and others.

Proof — Word used to describe the amount of alcohol in hard liquor. The proof number is twice the percentage of alcohol. For example, 80 proof whiskey would contain 40% alcohol.

Positive Self-Expectation — A feeling or a belief that you can do something worthwhile.

Recovering Alcoholic — Term used to describe an alcoholic who has chosen not to drink any more.

Sedative — A drug given to calm people down. Alcohol can be a sedative.

Skid Row — A place in towns and cities where "bums" are supposedly living. Most problem drinkers are not "skid row bums."

Sober — Not drunk or high; in complete control of one's words and actions.

Social Drinker — A person who drinks to relax or in social situations (dinner, celebrations, etc.) but not to the point where alcohol causes him or her any problems.

Stimulant — Often called an upper, a drug which speeds up the working of the central nervous system.

Tolerance — A condition where a person's system has become accustomed to a certain level of alcohol and therefore, needs more of it to get high or drunk each time.

Value — A strong feeling that something is important.

Bill Howells — Good-looking genius who wants to write crossword puzzles for the **New York Times** when he grows up.

Jamie Rattray — Tall, curly-haired boy wonder. Gives minimal input into creation of health books like this one, but makes a lot of money because he knows how to look busy.

Irv Seigler — Bearded twentieth-century philosopher and author of health books like this one.

Fritz Wasser — Modern artistic whiz with an addiction to india ink and Saturday morning cartoons.